This
Nature Storybook
belongs to:

Zoe

for all your hard work,
from Mrs Cullen

WALKER BOOKS

COMMA CATERPILLARS

ORANGE TIP CATERPILLARS

PEACOCK CATERPILLARS

It's impossible to say exactly when
you'll find caterpillars. It depends on where
you live, and what the weather's like, and all sorts
of other things. The eggs I found were laid in May.
They hatched out into caterpillars in June and changed
their skins four times during the next month or so. The first
three times I didn't see it happen, because they changed
inside their tents. But I did see the fourth time…
The caterpillar on the pea sticks pupated
in the middle of July and became
a butterfly in August.

For my grandfather, S.H.K., with love
V.F.
For Robert and Chloe
C.V.

First published 1993 by Walker Books Ltd
87 Vauxhall Walk, London SE11 5HJ

This edition published 2008

4 6 8 10 9 7 5

Text © 1993 Vivian French
Illustrations © 1993 Charlotte Voake

The right of Vivian French and Charlotte Voake to be identified as author and illustrator
respectively of this work has been asserted by them in accordance with the Copyright,
Designs and Patents Act 1988

This book has been typeset in Calligraphic 810 BT

Printed in China

British Library Cataloguing in Publication Data:
a catalogue record for this book is available from the British Library

ISBN 978-1-4063-1277-5

www.walker.co.uk

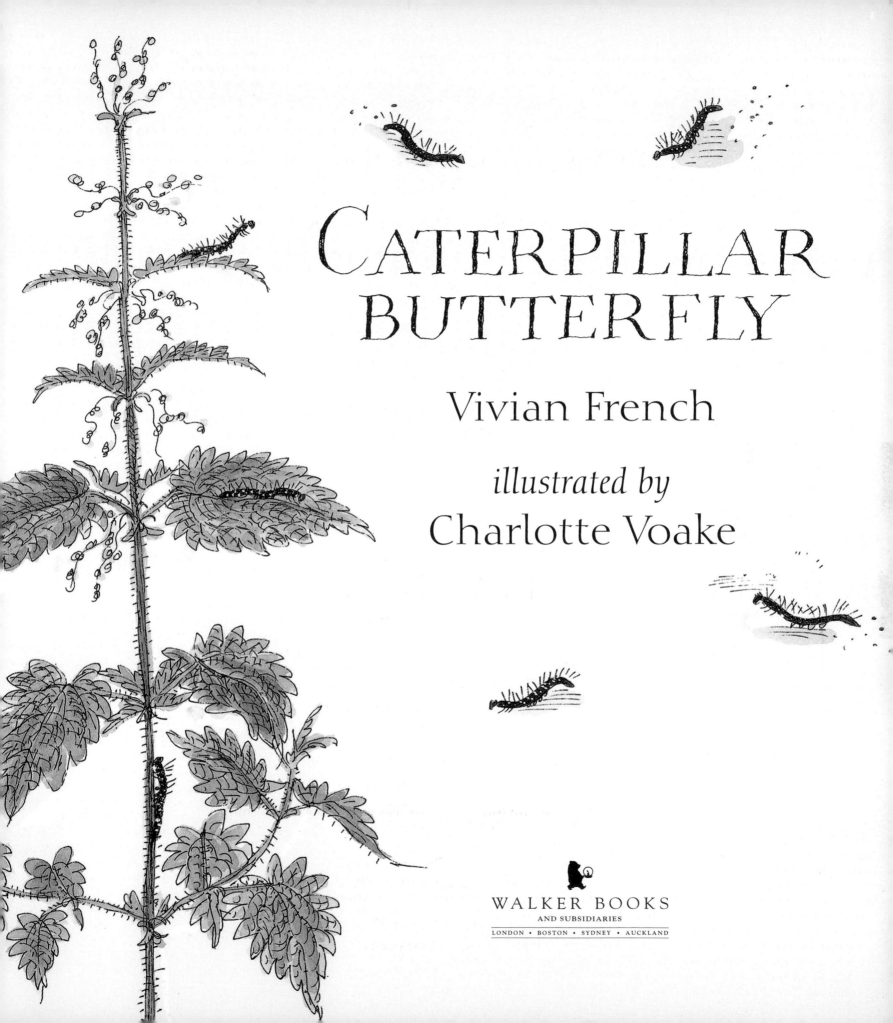

CATERPILLAR BUTTERFLY

Vivian French

illustrated by

Charlotte Voake

WALKER BOOKS

AND SUBSIDIARIES

LONDON · BOSTON · SYDNEY · AUCKLAND

My father and my grandfather both
liked gardening very much, but my
grandfather used to grow stinging nettles.
My father didn't; he said they were weeds,
and rooted them out.

"Why don't you get rid of your nettles?"
I asked my grandfather.

"Stinging nettles grow butterflies,"
he said. "Go and look."

I went and looked. I couldn't see any
butterflies, though. My grandfather turned
one of the nettle leaves over to show me
the bumps on the back of it, but I didn't
know what they were.

"Butterfly eggs," said my grandfather.

6

"What sort of butterflies?"

My grandfather peered closely at the bumps.

"Haven't got my specs on," he said, "but they could

be Tortoiseshells, or Peacocks. They both like nettles.

If you keep an eye on them you'll see when

the caterpillars hatch out."

"Won't they crawl away?" I asked.

My grandfather straightened up

and looked down at me.

"Humph," he said.

"You just keep watching."

So I did.

NETTLES WILL STING YOU IF YOU TOUCH THEM, BUT THEY WON'T STING THE CATERPILLARS.

THE EGGS ARE
DOME-SHAPED,
WITH LITTLE
RIDGES.
EACH EGG
IS ABOUT THE
SIZE OF THE
TOP
OF A PIN.

MOST
BUTTERFLIES
LAY THEIR EGGS
IN ONES AND TWOS,
MOVING FROM
PLANT TO PLANT.
PEACOCK AND
TORTOISESHELL
BUTTERFLIES
LAY LOTS OF
EGGS AT ONCE.

Nothing happened at all for
two days. It rained very hard
on the second day, but the
eggs were quite safe.

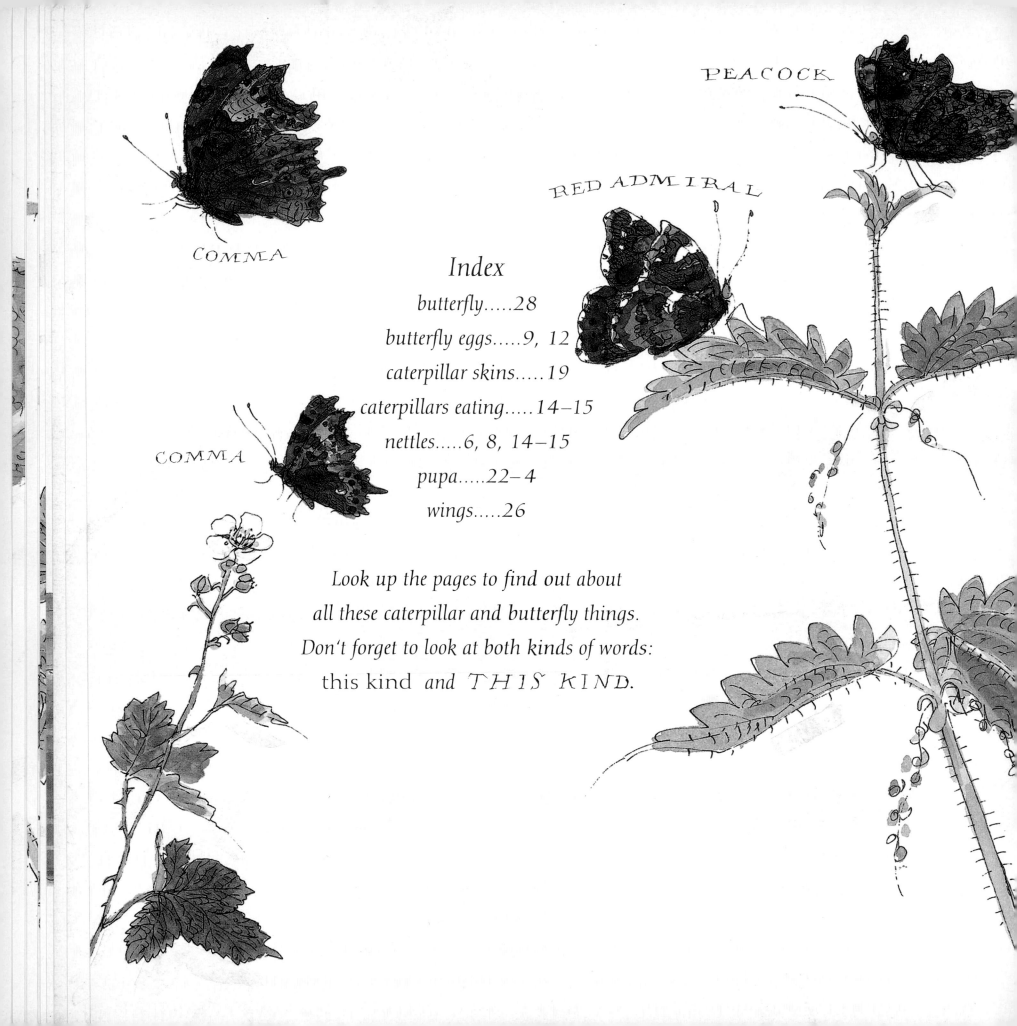

COMMA

PEACOCK

RED ADMIRAL

COMMA

Index

butterfly.....28

butterfly eggs.....9, 12

caterpillar skins.....19

caterpillars eating.....14–15

nettles.....6, 8, 14–15

pupa.....22–4

wings.....26

Look up the pages to find out about
all these caterpillar and butterfly things.
Don't forget to look at both kinds of words:
this kind and THIS KIND.

LARGE WHITE

ORANGE TIP

ORANGE TIP

COMMON BLUE

COMMON BLUE
CATERPILLAR

Praise for Nature Storybooks...

"For the child who constantly asks How? Why?
and What For? this series is excellent."
The Sunday Express

"A boon to parents seeking non-fiction picture books to read
with their children. They have excellent texts
and a very high standard of illustration to go with them."
The Daily Telegraph

"As books to engage and delight children, they work superbly.
I would certainly want a set in any primary
classroom I was working in."
Times Educational Supplement

"Here are books that stand out from the crowd,
each one real and individual in its own right and
the whole lot as different from most other series non-fiction
as tasty Lancashire is from processed Cheddar."
Books for Keeps

Find notes for teachers about how to use Nature Storybooks in the classroom at
www.walker.co.uk

Nature Storybooks support KS 1-2 Science